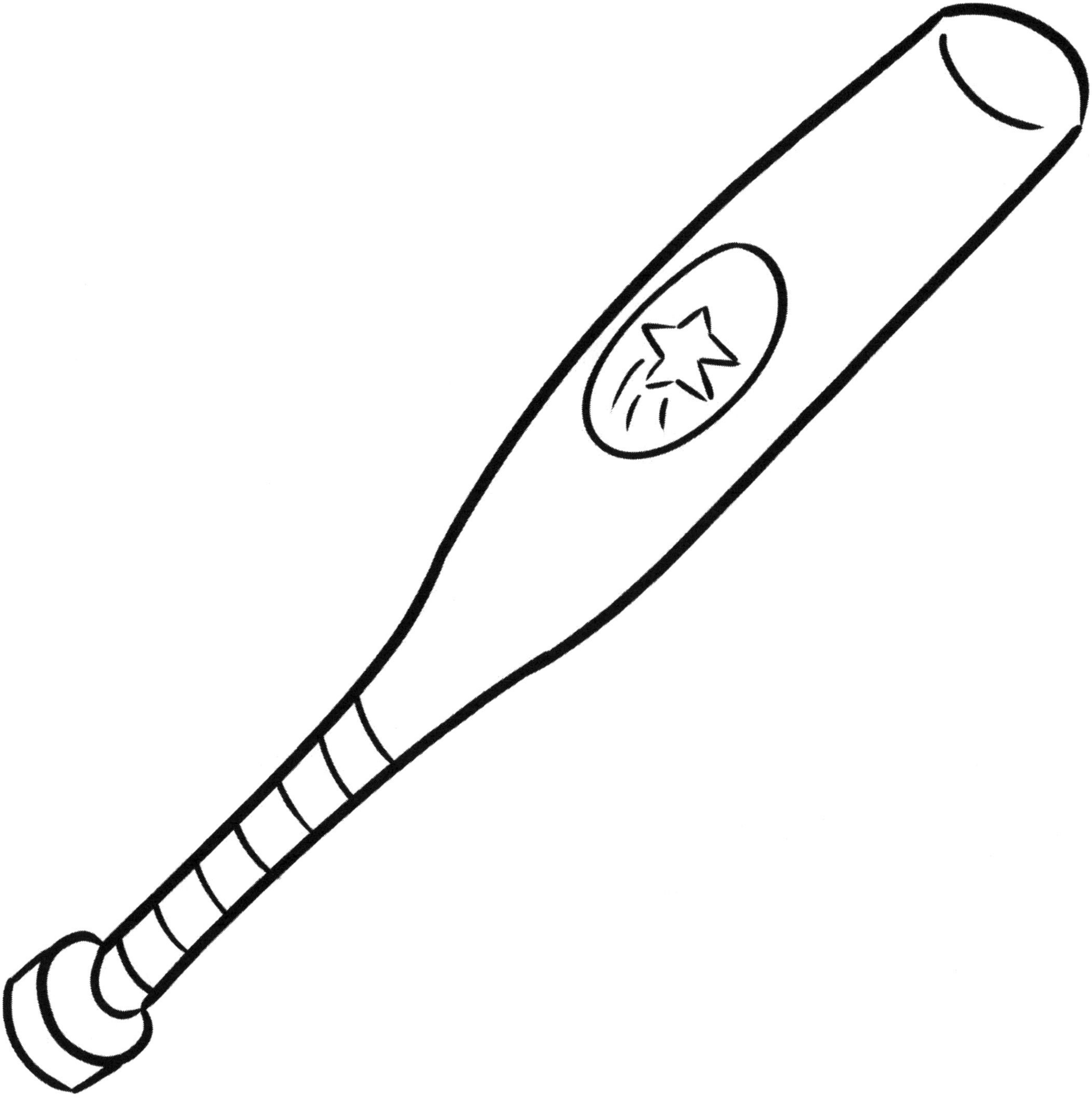

#1
BASEBAll

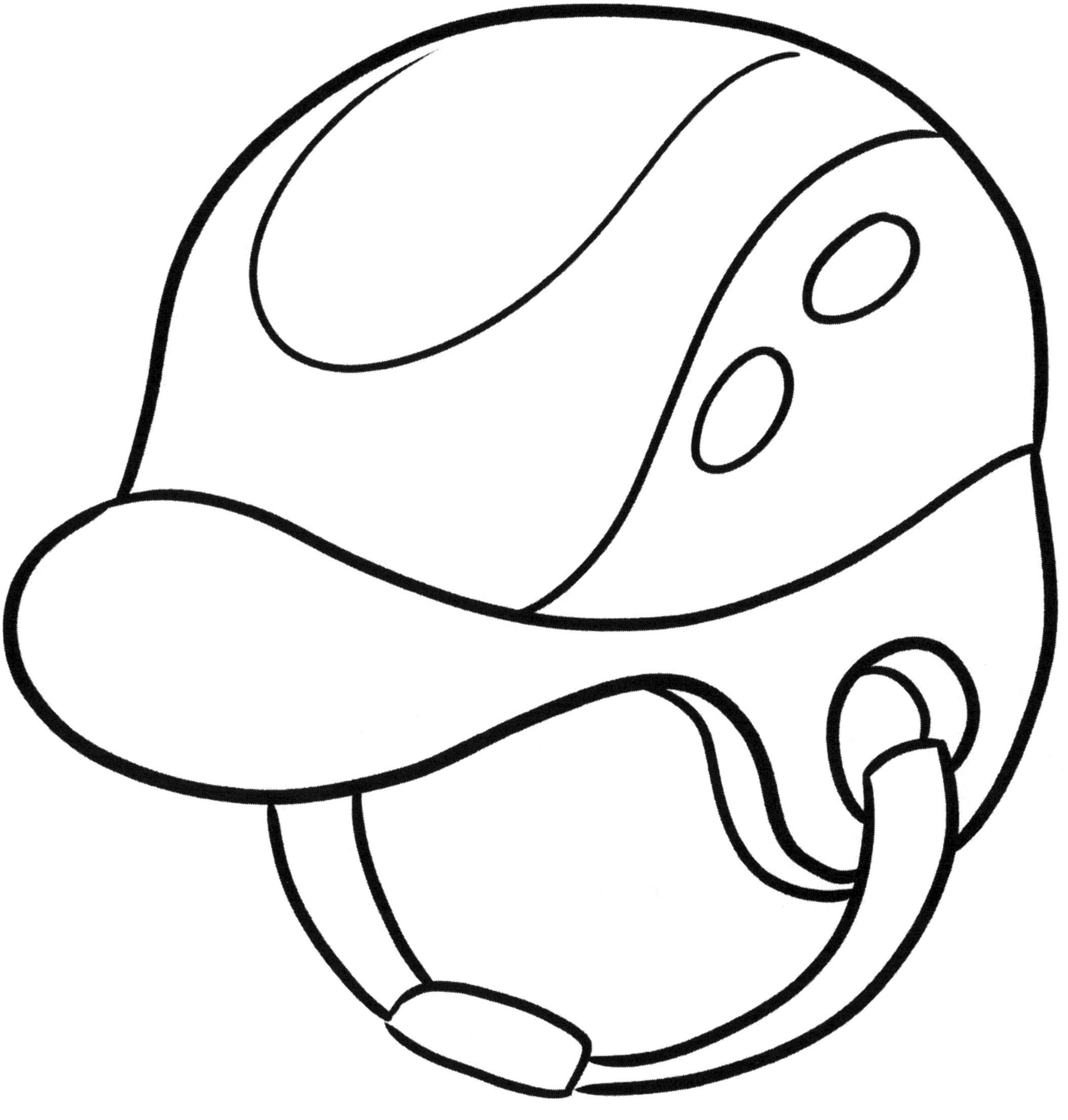

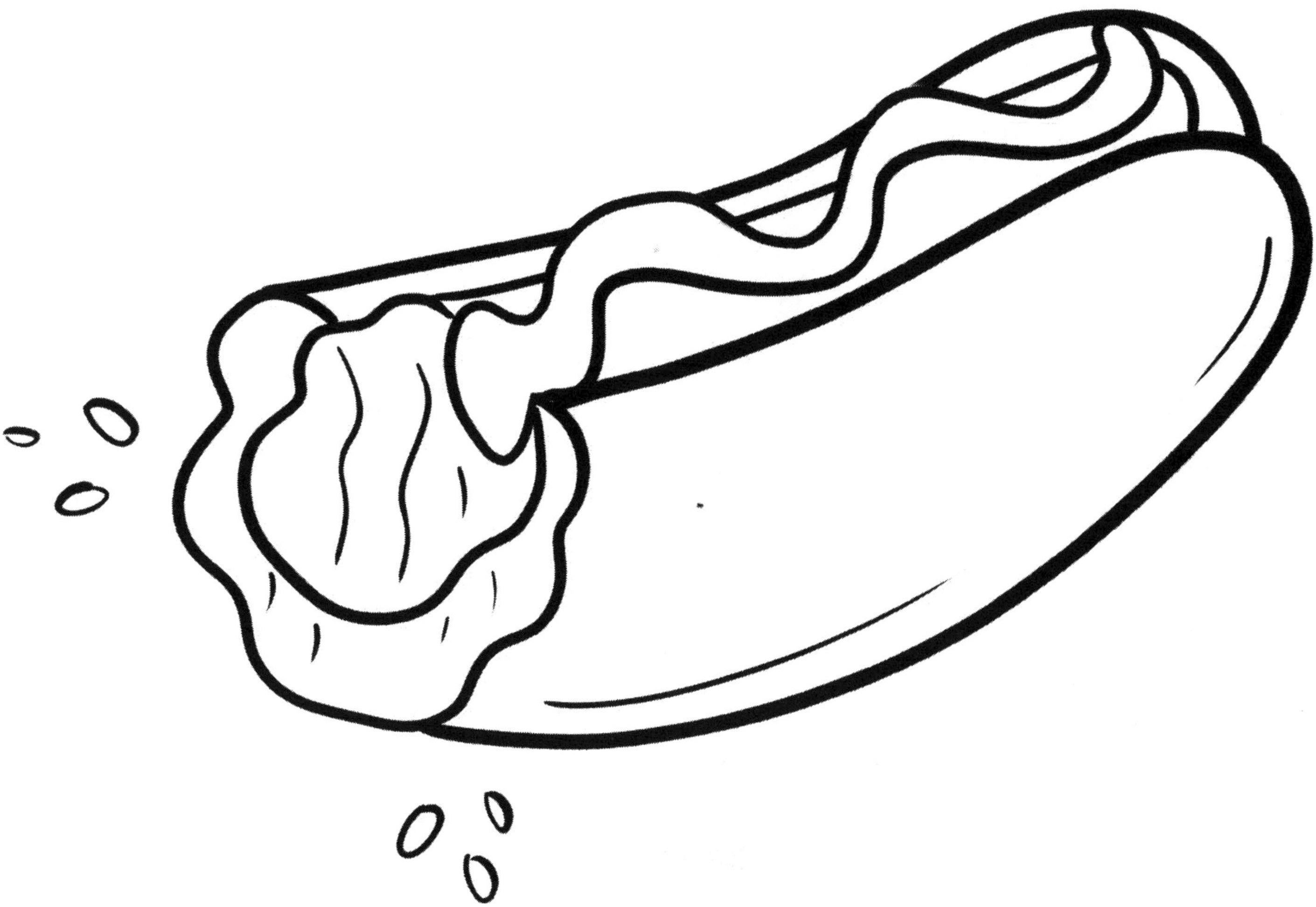

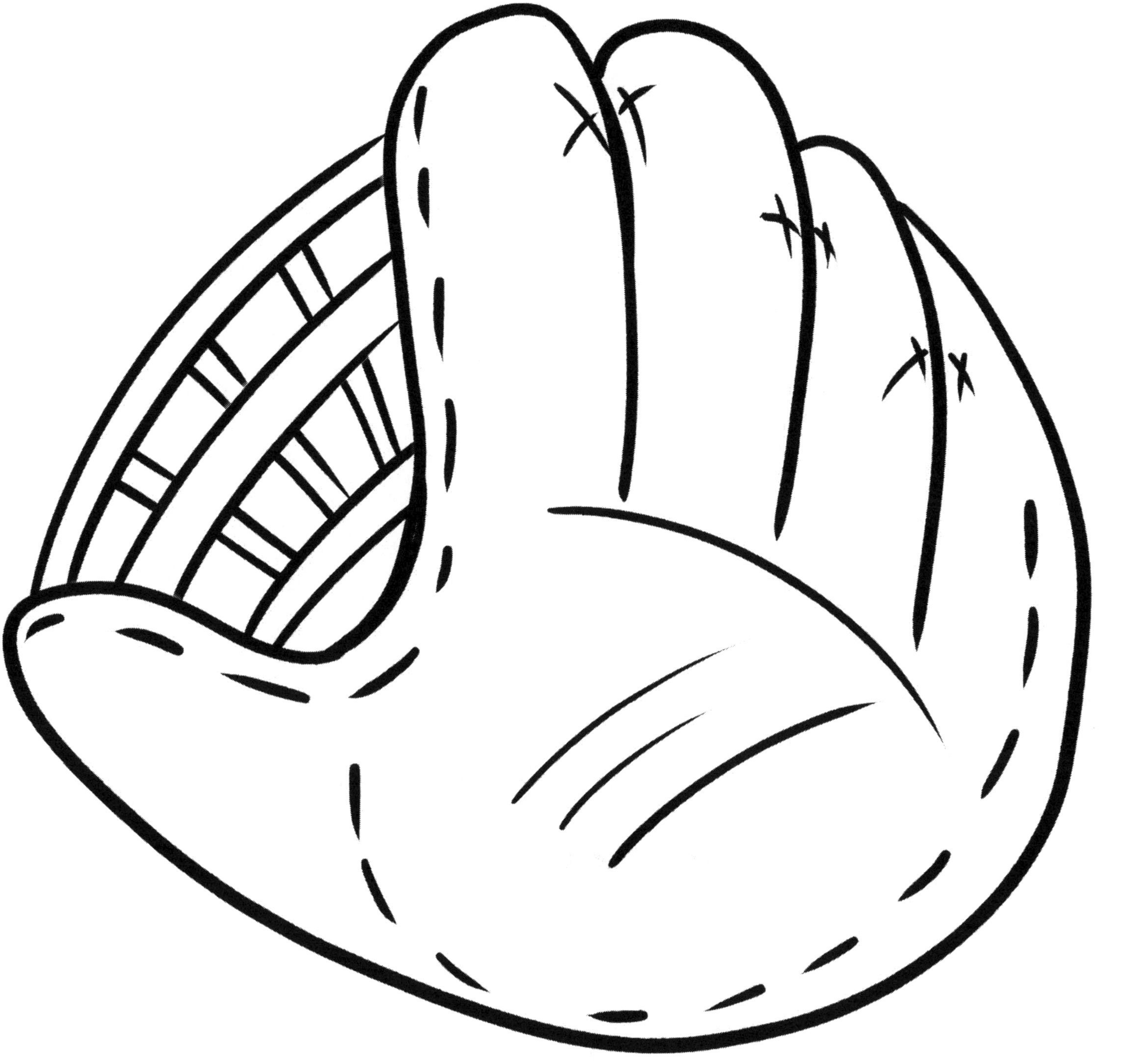

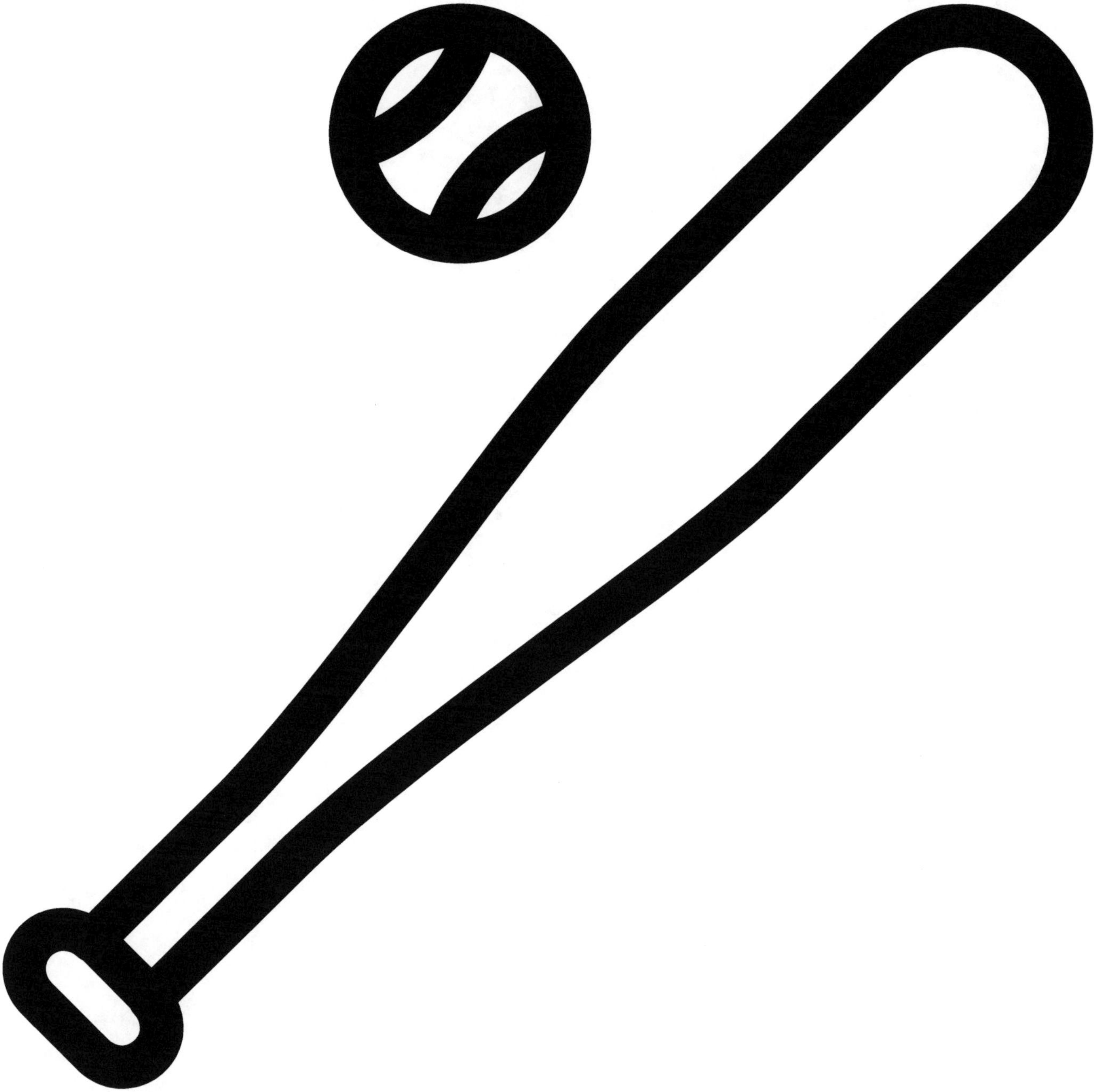

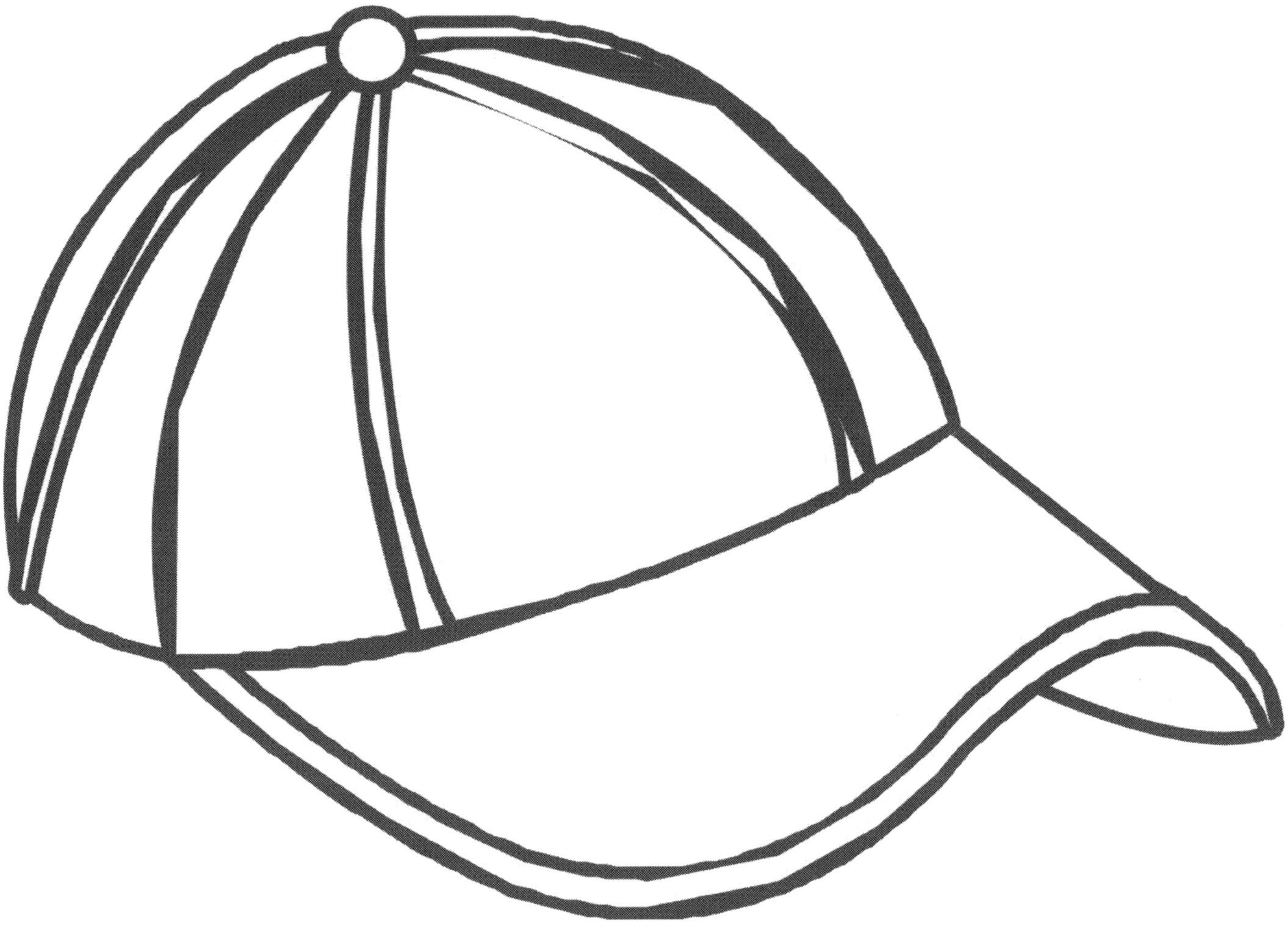

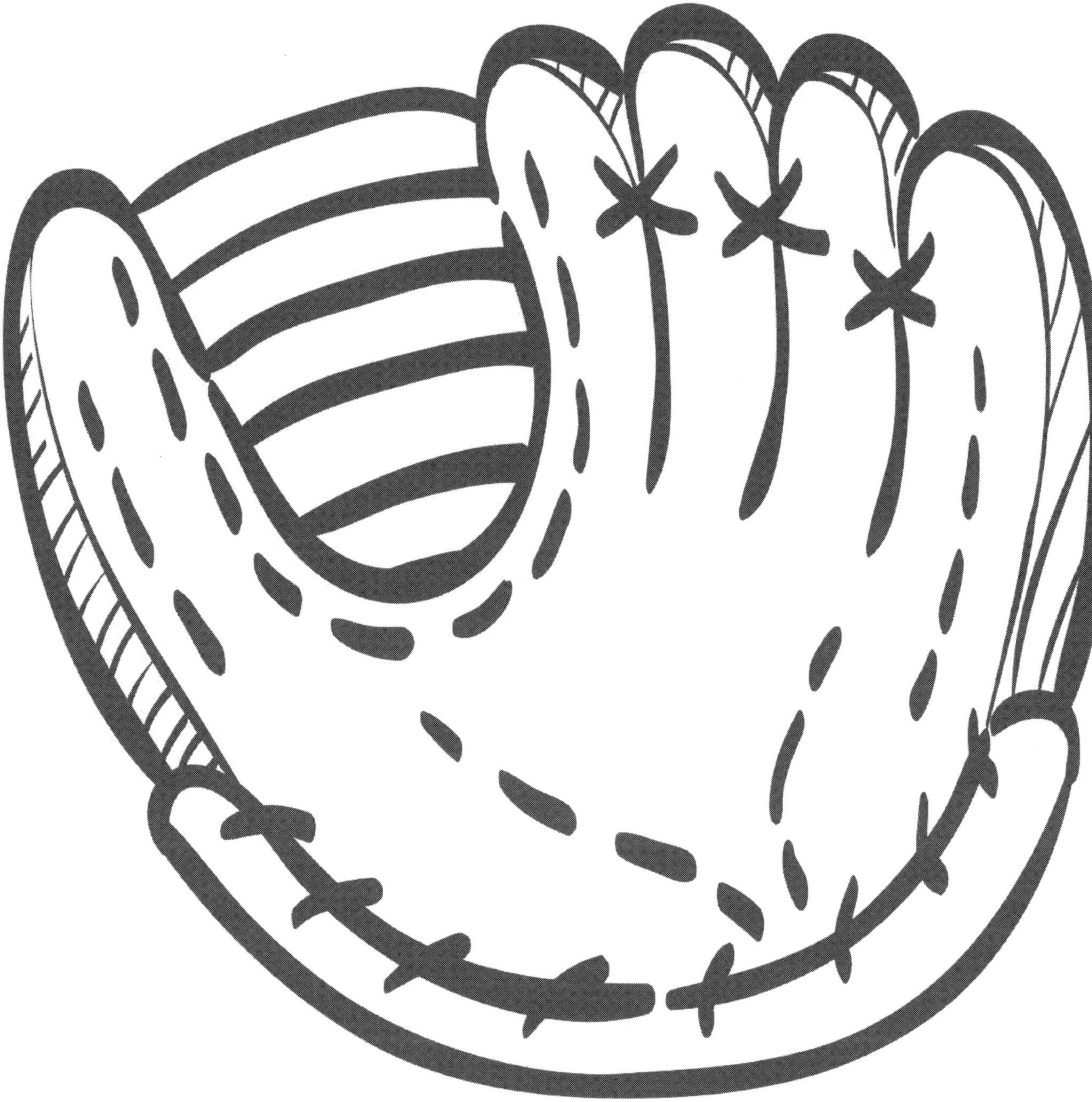

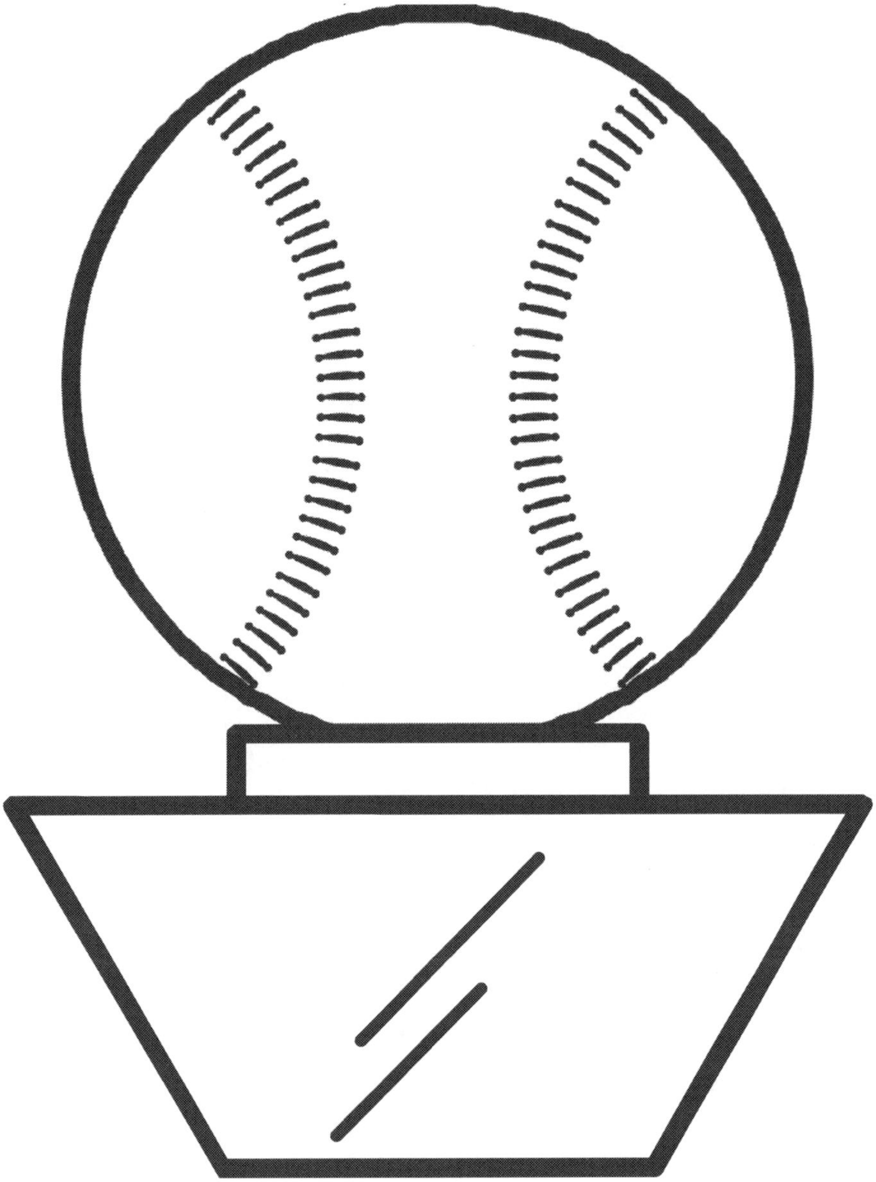

Made in the USA
Middletown, DE
15 July 2025

10691160R00024